GUINEA PIGS

THE ESSENTIAL GUIDE TO OWNERSHIP, CARE, & TRAINING FOR YOUR PET

Kate H. Pellham

© 2015

DISCLAIMER

TABLE OF CONTENTS

Chapter 1: Physical & Behavioral Traits of Guinea Pigs

As with dogs, cats, and any other type of pet, there are many different breeds that each have their own unique physical and behavioral characteristics. They are each adorable and lovable in their own way.

The one that suits you will depend on what you like and what kind of personality you want your pet to have. When it comes to guinea pigs, there are 10 popular breeds that are all unique. We'll take a brief look at each of them in this chapter.

In general, all guinea pigs are fairly social. They like a lot of attention and playtime. They are also usually happier if they've got a guinea pig friend to hang out with (although their friend should be the same sex in order to avoid your home being overrun by little guinea pigs)!

While they are social and usually relatively calm and docile around humans, it's still important to either get them at a very young age or to get one that was handled a lot by humans from infancy. They need some time to get used to humans.

Physically, guinea pigs range from 1 ½ to 2 ½ pounds and will grow to between 8 and 10 inches. They generally live between 5 to 7 years and become sexually mature after just 3-5 weeks of age. They can also become pregnant year round and have short gestation periods.

With that in mind, let's start looking at the unique characteristics of each of the 10 most popular breeds of guinea pig:

The American

As you might have guessed from the name, this is the most popular breed in the United States. If you are picturing a guinea pig in your head right now, it is probably an American guinea pig.

They have light brown or golden fur with white patches on the face and tummy. They are known for being particularly calm and docile.

American guinea pigs get along especially well with other guinea pigs and are one of the best options for children—although it is still important that your child understands how to handle and play with the guinea pig without harming or scaring it.

They have shorter hair than other guinea pig breeds which means they don't require quite as much grooming. This is ideal for children or first-time pet owners who aren't yet used to caring for a pet.

The Abyssinian

This is one of the oldest breeds of guinea pig out there. Their hair is longer than an American guinea pig but still not as long as other breeds. The hair—which can come in a range of colors from dark brown to white—looks sort of like they have perpetual bedhead.

The longer hair means more grooming is required and they especially like to get into trouble so they may not be the ideal pet for a young child. But they are perfect for the adult who wants an irresistibly adorable pet with a personality leaning more on the adorably naughty side.

Abyssinian guinea pigs are also one of the breeds you'll see regularly at pet shows. So if you are interested in grooming a star, you should definitely consider getting an Abyssinian. Make sure to spend extra time on grooming and ensuring a highly nutritious diet if that's what your plans are.

The Peruvian

This is one of the most striking guinea pigs when it comes to appearance. They have the longest hair of any guinea pig breed. Their luscious locks are perfectly straight which can make them look like a walking wig in the cutest way possible. It can grow up to 20 inches long!

Some owners will cut the hair to minimize time spent grooming. If you choose to keep it long, you'll definitely need to brush your guinea pig on a daily basis. Otherwise, the hair will get tangled and this can make the guinea pig uncomfortable. Not to mention, they will start to look like a walking bird's nest instead of a wig.

In terms of personality, the Peruvian guinea pig tends to be more curious and alert about its surroundings than other breeds. This curiosity makes them less timid and more social. They'll run to greet you purely out curiosity to see who you are and what you're about.

This makes them a good option for children and first-time pet owners. Although, it's recommended to keep their hair trimmed in this case since a child or first-time owner may not remember to groom them on a daily basis.

The Silkie

The silkie has hair on the longer side as well although it's not nearly as long and flowy as the Peruvian. The hair on their head also hangs differently. Instead of draping around their face as it does with the Peruvian, the silkie's hair sweeps back as if it had been slicked back and styled.

As with the Peruvian, though, this guinea pig requires daily brushing to prevent tangling and discomfort. But if you're prepared for that, it can actually be a pretty calming and meditative activity that both you and your guinea pig will enjoy.

Because of their grooming needs, they aren't recommended for children unless you are willing to take on some of the responsibility for caring for the pet—or you are able to be diligent in reminding and supervising your child in order to make sure the silkie is getting the proper grooming it requires.

Grooming needs aside, they do make wonderfully cuddly pets that your child—and you!—will certainly enjoy.

The Teddy

The teddy is aptly named as its fur gives it the appearance of being a tiny teddy bear. The fur is short and very dense so that if fluffs up much like on a teddy bear. Their coats usually are more on the wiry side so they aren't quite as soft and luxurious as a Peruvian or Silkie might be. But they are still totally pettable and adorable.

One of the biggest plusses for the teddy is that it requires minimal grooming compared to other breeds. They will need occasional brushing since their wiry fur has a tendency to cling to bits and pieces—think big bushy beard with food scraps clinging to it.

When it comes to personality, the teddy is one of the best guinea pigs on the market. They are energetic and friendly. They are also known for warming up to humans relatively quickly. This combined with the low maintenance makes them the absolute best choice for children.

The Texel

The Texel is one of the most unique breeds in terms of physical appearance. Their long hair has soft curls which give them that perfect beach wave look. They are one of the most sought after breeds by guinea pig enthusiasts and are a common star of guinea pig pet shows.

Unfortunately, their luscious curls also make them one of the higher maintenance breeds of guinea pigs. Their hair is extremely prone to tangling so they need to be brushed at least once per day but it's recommended to do it twice.

They also need regular baths and ear cleanings because the excess fur makes the prone to earwax buildup. Taken all together, this breed definitely requires the most grooming.

It's also recommended to use fleece bedding instead of shredded paper or sawdust to minimize the amount of debris that gets into the coat.

If you're willing and able to manage the grooming needs, the Texel will reward you with its amazingly sweet and adoring personality. It loves to be groomed and loves spending time with its human owners.

The White Crested

The white crested guinea pig is a short-haired breed with a white "crown" of hair on the top of its head. The rest of its body is dark brown or grayish.

They are relatively low maintenance as a result of their shorter hair and resemble the American—both in physical appearance and in personality.

They have bubbly, sociable personalities that make them great for those who want a pet they can play with often. If you don't have the time to give it regular attention, though, you may want to consider a more docile and mild-mannered breed. These guys love to run around and play as much as possible.

Since they love to play and don't require excessive grooming, they are a good option for children. Although they probably won't be winning any shows.

The Rex

The rex guinea pig is also a short-haired breed and somewhat resembles the teddy with its fluffy, wooly coat. It's not as soft as a teddy's fur, though. But its unique texture is still enjoyable to pet. Their ears are also longer and droopier, similar to a dog's ears.

They have a well-tempered personality and enjoy being handled and pet. As long as your children are old enough to know how to handle the pet gently, the rex can be a great first pet for them.

The minimal grooming required and the docile temperament make them great starter pets. Just make sure they aren't getting handled roughly or played with to vigorously. They like to play but let them guide the playtime activities.

The Himalayan

The Himalayan guinea pig is often nicknamed the "Siamese cat" of guinea pigs. This is because of its fur pattern and texture. The soft fur is a creamy white color throughout the body with accents of black fur on the ears, nose, and paws—just like a Siamese cat.

They do better in cool and mild climates since excess heat or sunlight can not only harm the guinea pig's health but also cause the dark accents around the ears, nose, and paws to fade and disappear.

Aside from their need for a milder climate, they are relatively low maintenance. Their fur is short and they are well-mannered.

The Skinny Pig

Unlike the other 9 breeds of guinea pig, the skinny pig is almost completely hairless. It does have some tufts on its nose, feet, and legs but for the most part, it is totally hair free.

Without the long, radiant hair, they definitely are the most conventionally attractive breed of guinea pig but they do have their own unique sort of charm that does appeal to some people.

If you need a pet that is fluffy and adorable in the typical sense, this is not the one for you. But if you love pets that are unique and sure to be a good conversation starter, the skinny pig might be just what you are looking for.

They are just as loving, playful, and energetic as any other breed of guinea pig and will surely appreciate a caring, happy home. Plus, there's no brushing required!

Chapter 2: Guinea Pigs as Pets

You've read about the 10 different adorable breeds of guinea pig and their characteristics but what is it really like to have one of them as a pet?

As with owning any pet, there are certain advantages and disadvantages. Caring for any life means responsibility but it also means having an adorable furry friend that loves and adores you.

Your ability to balance the advantages and disadvantages will depend entirely on you and your current situation. In this chapter, we'll lay out the key pros and cons of owning a guinea pig as a pet.

This way, you'll be able to decide whether or not those pros and cons work with your needs, wants, and abilities. Let's start on a positive note by discussing some of the wonderful benefits of raising a guinea pig.

The Pros of Owning a Pet Guinea Pig

Here are a few of the biggest benefits of choosing a guinea pig to be your new pet:

Friendly & Playful

One of the issues with most small, cage pets—hamsters, rabbits, rats, and so on—is that they are not naturally the most social species you'll find. With enough handling and training, they will get used to and start to enjoy your company but if you don't have the time or energy to really put in the effort to socialize them, they will be pretty skittish and unfriendly.

Guinea pigs, on the other hand, are naturally very social creatures. So much so, in fact, that they even do better with a guinea pig friend rather than on their own. They are friendly, playful, and energetic.

They are also more docile and less likely to bite. While you do need to start handling them from a young age so that they become comfortable with humans, it doesn't take as much effort as it does with other pets.

It's also very child-friendly as a result of its social and playful personality. They will be much more tolerant around young children. Although you still need to supervise and make sure the children aren't too rough as this could damage the guinea pig's health.

Nonviolent

As mentioned above, guinea pigs have a much calmer and friendlier temperament. They are less likely to bite, scratch, or run away than other pets.

This means they are relatively safe for children and great for first time pet owners who may not be as experienced in handling animals and helping them become comfortable around humans.

Of course, it's best to get your guinea pig while it's still young—or an older one that has already been handled often by humans—so that it is less afraid around you.

When feeling threatened, all animals will naturally try to defend themselves. The difference here is that guinea pigs are generally less timid so they don't feel threatened as easily as, say, hamsters or rabbits.

Low Starting Costs

Some pets can come with high starting costs. Fish for example need an aquarium, water filter, aquarium accessories, thermometers, lights, and electricity. And in the end, you don't even get to play with them. You just stare at them.

Guinea pigs have low start-up costs. If you buy everything, you can expect to spend somewhere between $150 and $200. However, if you are willing to get crafty, you can easily get those costs down below $100.

Because guinea pigs can't jump very high, it's actually fairly easy to make your own cage at home. Instead of store bought bedding, you can shred up old paper. You can easily make your own hiding box.

All in all, it's very easy and very cheap to get all the supplies you need. Then, the only regular costs you will have are food pellets and hay.

Of course, vet visits can get pricey but this is the case with any pet so if you're not prepared to cover vet costs, you should reconsider owning a pet at all.

Low Maintenance

As you've already read in the previous chapter, some breeds of guinea pig are lower maintenance than others. However, the species as a whole is still relatively low maintenance compared to other pets you might get.

Plus, even the high maintenance breeds are only considered "high maintenance" because you need to brush and groom them more often. But this grooming is also a great way to bond with your pet and can actually be a very enjoyable experience for both of you.

They are also low maintenance when it comes to feeding. You just need to get the manufactured guinea pig pellets. These contain all the nutrients they require.

A few times per week, you'll want to supplement their pellets with fresh vegetables—particularly vegetables with high vitamin C like carrots, tomatoes, and leafy greens. The vitamin C in their pellets breaks down and is lost quickly.

Since guinea pigs, like humans, are unable to produce their own vitamin C in their bodies, they need to get all of their daily requirements from their diet.

If you are unable to feed them fresh veggies regularly, you can also buy a vitamin C powder which you simply sprinkle on top of their pellets.

Aside from feeding and hygiene, there's not much else you need to do to keep your guinea pig healthy. It will thrive much, much better (and be a more enjoyable pet) if you play with it regularly but if you miss a day of playtime, you won't cause permanent damage to your pet's health.

Stress Management

Pets are great for stress management. The cuddlier they are, the better and guinea pigs are one of the cuddliest and most affectionate pets you'll find.

Petting, grooming, and playing with your pet guinea pig will naturally reduce your stress levels which will improve your overall health just as you are improving your guinea pig's health.

If you have a high-stress lifestyle, coming home to a happy, bubbly guinea pig can be the perfect way to wind down and decompress.

Your new guinea pig can decrease your risk for heart disease, lower your blood pressure, lower your risk for obesity and diabetes, and help you manage depression and anxiety.

So if any of those are risk factors in your life, I would say a guinea pig is well worth all of the negatives you are going to read about in the next section!

The Cons of Owning a Pet Guinea Pig

Here are the primary disadvantages to owning a guinea pig that you need to know about before you make a smart decision about whether or not to own one:

Need More Attention & Exercise than other Pets

While a hamster might be able to spend days running around its cage or inside its hamster wheel, a guinea pig needs to be let out so that it can stretch its legs and exercise.

While most pets need a certain degree of attention and exercise, it can be problematic with a guinea pig because it's up to you to remember to give it that attention and exercise.

When a cat or dog needs exercise, it can just choose to get up and run around or play. When they want your attention, they can come sit on your lap (or your keyboard) and show you that they want you to give them attention.

Your guinea pig, on the other hand, is sitting in a cage. It has limited space to really run around and play. More importantly, it can't just get up and walk over to you when it wants your attention.

This means that you really need to put the effort into remembering to let your guinea pig out of its cage and hanging out with it. It's entirely up to you to make sure that it's getting the attention and exercise that it needs.

So, while it may not necessarily need more or less than another pet, it just doesn't have the ability to let you know what it needs and when as easily as a pet that doesn't require a cage.

Costs Can Add Up

Guinea pigs are definitely one of the more affordable pets out there. General costs (food and hay) are going to run you around $20 per month. This isn't so bad.

However, you have to factor in the occasional costs of going to the vet, replacing old toys, and possibly grooming (if you don't do it yourself).

Over the course of the year, these can add up. And it's a good idea to set aside a little money each month to put toward emergency vet costs just in case your little furry friend needs some unexpected medical attention.

Without putting aside money for these vet costs, you might find yourself having to make tough decisions about whether or not you can afford to get your pet the help it needs.

Of course, this is the case with all pets so it's not so much a specific disadvantage that comes with owning guinea pigs as with owning any pet at all. If you're not prepared to take on these costs, you may not be ready to own any pet—with the possible exception of fish.

Noise

This point can go either way. Some people find the sound guinea pigs make to be adorable. Others find it irritating. In either case, they can get quite noisy although they are rarely noisy throughout the entire day.

The main issue here is that guinea pigs can be active during the day and the night. So if it's feeling active and energetic in the middle of the night, it could become quite noisy right when you are trying to sleep.

You can minimize the chances of being woken up by loud guinea pig squeals in the night by making an extra effort to get the guinea pig on your schedule. Let it get a lot of exercise during the day and play with it often while you are awake. This way, by nightfall, it will be tuckered out and ready for bed.

Smell

Because guinea pigs live in cages and can get those cages pretty messy, they tend to leave a distinct odor in your house. However, this odor is most notable when the cage needs to be cleaned. So, as long as you do regular cage cleanings, you'll avoid any overpowering stench.

Visitors to your home may be able to detect a faint smell but, as long as the cage is clean, it shouldn't ever become intolerable.

But if you have a particularly sensitive nose, you might better off with a clean, cage-free animal like a cat.

Need Large Cage

While other small caged pets like rats or hamsters can get by with relatively limited cage space, guinea pigs need quite a bit of room to feel comfortable and happy.

This is particulary because they can't use those rotating hamster wheels that allow them to run around in one place. These are dangerous for guinea pigs so they need to be able to run around on their own.

The larger cage will help provide more space for movement but you'll also have to take it out of its cage on a regular basis in order to make sure it can run around freely.

Long Term Commitment

The average life span of a guinea pig is between 5 to 7 years but it is definitely not uncommon for a guinea pig to live up to 10 years.

This means they are a long term commitment especially when compared to a fish or hamster which typically live just 1-2 years. So if your life is not currently stable or you aren't ready to commit to a pet for the long term, you may want to opt for no pet or a pet with a much shorter lifespan.

Chapter 3: Guinea Pig Necessities

Once you've decided whether or not you actually want a pet guinea pig and which breed suits you the best, the next most important step is to stock up on all the necessary supplies your guinea pig is going to need to make him or herself at home in your house.

The supplies needed to keep a guinea pig happy and healthy are fairly basic and affordable. All in all, the supplies discussed in this chapter (including both basic and nonessential) will run you less than $200.

If you are extremely frugal and crafty, you can get it covered for under $100—that's assuming you construct your own cage, playpen, hiding box, and so on. So if you're budget is tight, don't feel like a guinea pig is out of your reach.

Just look around your house and see what supplies you already have that could be repurposed and reused to take care of your guinea pig. The most important thing is that you make sure you are able to take care of the regular maintenance costs.

You'll have to buy food and hay on a regular basis. This should cost less than $20 per month altogether. So read on and learn about what you'll need for your new pet guinea pig.

Basic Supplies

Below, you'll find the absolute essentials. These are the supplies you can't get away without having. Your guinea pig needs these in order to be healthy and happy.

A Cage

A single guinea pig needs a minimum of 7 ½ square feet of cage space. This is so that it has space to run as well as space for a food dish, hiding box, and other supplies.

The floor should be made of a solid material like plastic rather than wire grating. A wire floor can hurt the guinea pig's feet.

You cannot use an aquarium as this does not allow for enough breathability. A wire cage is best.

Hiding Box

In addition to having its own cage, a guinea pig needs a hiding box. If you've got 2 guinea pigs in one cage, you need 2 hiding boxes.

They may not use it often but they do value the option of having their private space when they need it. These are relatively cheap at the store. But you can also make them yourself out of old plastic Tupperware or wood.

The important thing is that it is not transparent and not made out of toxic material as the guinea pig may chew on it at times.

Food Dish

You can't just dump the pellets directly into the bedding of the cage. You'll need to use a food dish so that it stay clean and separate from any urine and feces covered bedding.

You should also clean this dish regularly and make sure that it stays dry. This doesn't have to be a specialized guinea pig food dish. It can be any small bowl as long as it doesn't have any toxic coating or materials in it.

Water Bottle

You'll need to get a water bottle for the cage that your guinea pig can drink from. Some people will use a water dish but this spills easily and ruins the bedding which means you'll need to clean the cage more often.

The water bottle prevents spillage so that you don't have to refill as often or clean up wet bedding so often. They only cost a few dollars and it is well worth the investment.

Bedding

The bottom of the cage needs to be filled with dry bedding that the guinea pig can dig around in. This will be one of your regular costs as you need to change it about once a week.

But, luckily, you don't need to pay for the store bought stuff. You can simply use old shredded up paper. The important thing is that you keep it dry and replace it regularly. Don't use glossy paper.

As an alternative to paper bedding, you can also use fleece bedding which can be washed and reused. This is recommended for breeds that have long hair as it will minimize the amount of junk that gets stuck to their fur.

Food

The guinea pig diet is pretty simple. They can survive on exclusively pellets (as long as you add vitamin C powder to it) or a mixture of pellets and fresh vegetables that are high in vitamin C.

The important thing is to make sure they get enough vitamin C in their diet because their bodies cannot produce this vitamin by itself so they are at a high risk for vitamin C deficiency if you aren't careful.

They can eat fruits on occasion. Fresh fruit is the best option to use as treats when you are training your guinea pig. Avoid the store bought guinea pig treats as these have a lot of sugar and are often made with yogurt which is difficult for your pet to digest.

Timothy Hay

It is a little-known fact that guinea pigs need hay as a regular part of their diet. This is entirely separate from the pellets, vegetables and fruits you feed it.

The hay serves two important purposes. First, it acts as a digestive aid to help their stomachs break down and absorb the food they eat.

Secondly, chewing the hay helps grind down their molars. This is important because guinea pig teeth are constantly growing. Without a means of grinding their teeth down, they will become too long which can cause serious health problems.

The hay you find at the store is usually alfalfa hay. This is good for newborns and pregnant guinea pigs but should not be used as their regular hay.

Alfalfa hay is rich in calcium and other minerals which, while necessary, can cause bladder stones if eaten in excess. This is why you need to specifically ask for timothy hay and make sure your guinea pig has a constant supply of it.

Nail Clippers

You will need to trim your guinea pig's nails every 4 to 6 weeks. As they grow, they will curl backward and can grow into the pad of your pet's paw. This is painful and can cause a serious infection.

You can use regular nail clippers so there's no need to buy special guinea pig clippers. If you're worried about hurting your guinea pig, you can take your pet to the vet for the first trimming and have the vet teach you how to do it on your own.

You can also find tutorials online. It's not very difficult to do and once you've done it the first time, you'll have no trouble doing it anytime after. It will only get easier as your guinea pig grows to trust you more and more.

Non-Essential Supplies

Here are some extra supplies that are highly recommended for your guinea pig but not strictly necessary to its health and survival. Getting them will, however, make it much happier and improve its chances of living a long, happy life.

Pet Pen

A pet pen is an optional item you can use to create a little play area inside your house or out in your yard so that your guinea pig can run around and play outside of its cage without getting lost.

This is highly recommended especially for large houses or homes with a lot of nooks and crannies that your guinea pig might be able to get stuck in.

You don't need to buy a special pet pen, though. You can use any sort of fencing or structures to create a bounded area for your guinea pig. Just make sure it is taller than the height of your guinea pig when it stands on its hind legs. They cannot jump but they may be able to hoist themselves up and over the edge if they can get a grip on the top.

Toys

Toys are a great way to enrich your guinea pig's life and make it much happier. You can make sure that it can entertain itself even when you are not around to play with it.

There are many toys available at pet stores but you have to be careful. Safety standards for pet items are not as strict as they are for human products.

Here is a short list of safe items that your guinea pig will enjoy playing with:

- Short sections of thick PVC pipe

- Terra Cotta flower pots

- Cardboard boxes (without glue, staples, plastic, or a glossy cover)

- Wooden blocks (the same as you'd give to a baby)

- Tennis balls

- Squeaky toys (chew safe type)

A special note about your guinea pig supplies: do not get it a hamster wheel. Guinea pigs have a very fragile bone structure which cannot withstand the stress that would be put on it by a hamster wheel. These are not safe for guinea pigs. The same goes for hamster balls.

Your guinea pig is not a hamster. Let it run around and get exercise the natural way so that it doesn't place unusual strain on its bone structure.

Chew Toys

Chew toys are another way to help your guinea pig keep its teeth ground down. These can be balls, pieces of wood, blocks, or even stuffed animals. You can also get special chew sticks at the store if you feel like it.

These keep your guinea pig entertained and healthy as it helps them keep their teeth ground to a healthy size. You should take note that a guinea pig loves to chew so chances are it will turn just about everything into a chew toy.

Make sure that there is nothing in the cage that is toxic or unsafe for your guinea pig to chew on. If you give it a stuffed animal, keep an eye on it to make sure it's not ripping out the stuffing. It may try to eat this which is unhealthy.

Chapter 4: The Basics of Guinea Pig Care

Now that you know what the different kinds of guinea pig breeds are like, what it's like to own one as a pet, and the supplies you'll need to keep it happy, it's time to dive into the basic care you'll need to provide for your new pet.

This includes keeping up the cage, feeding, and cleaning your guinea pig. We'll also talk about toys and playtime which, while technically optional, are highly recommended and also happen to make guinea pig ownership way more fun!

At the end of the chapter, you'll get a brief overview of the different health problems that are most likely to occur in guinea pigs.

Housing

As mentioned in the previous chapter, a guinea pig should have at least a 7 ½ square foot cage. For each additional guinea pig you add to the same cage, add another 3 ½ square feet, minimum.

This is important. Even if someone at a pet store tells you that the smaller cage is fine, they are wrong. Guinea pigs are one of the largest caged pets you can own and they need space to move around.

If the cage is too small, they'll hardly have enough room for a sleeping area and a toilet area. They are particular about keeping separate activities designated to separate areas so if the toilet area is too close to the food or bed area, they will get unhappy. Just as you would if you had to use the toilet in the same room that you eat your food!

As for maintenance, here are the general rules to follow:

1. Daily: check for really dirty or wet spots and replace those spots with fresh bedding if you find any.

2. Weekly: dump out the bedding and replace with fresh bedding. Clean out the food bowl.

3. Monthly: do a full, deep cleaning. Replace bedding and water. Clean the food dish. Rinse the water bottle and use a pet-safe disinfectant to scrub down the cage.

Food & Water

Your guinea pig can survive on pellets alone as long as you add vitamin C powder but it will be much happier with a more varied diet. Just like you, they get bored eating the same thing day in and day out.

Below you will get a list of guinea pig safe foods to feed your pet. Try to add in one or two each day if possible. It doesn't have to be a lot—a lettuce leaf or baby carrot each day is fine. Just make sure it has some variety.

Before we get to that list, let's talk about the basic guidelines for food and water:

1. Get pellets specifically formulated for Guinea pigs. It should have no seeds or dried fruit added. It should be fortified with vitamin C (otherwise by a vitamin C only powder supplement to sprinkle on it).

2. Make sure they always have timothy hay available.

3. Refresh water daily. During particularly hot weather, replace it more often so they always have cool water.

4. Do not use vitamin drops for water. Most vitamins dissolve in water so it's pointless. Plus, they only need vitamin C supplemented. If they get other vitamins supplemented, you risk reaching toxic levels of those other vitamins.

Now that you have the basic rules, here are the veggies you should try to feed your guinea pig regularly:

- Grass (pesticide and chemical free)
- Broccoli
- Cabbage
- Carrot
- Celery
- Spinach
- Cucumber
- Bell Pepper (seeds removed)

- Kale

- Celery

- Dandelion Leaves

- Tomatoes

- Parsley

- Pear

- Grapes (seedless)

- Apple

All fruits and veggies should be given to them raw. Fruits should be given sparingly. Use them primarily as treats, not as a regular food source.

Hygiene

The hygiene routine will depend very much on the breed of guinea pig you have. The rules below are guidelines for shorter haired guinea pigs. If you have long haired breeds, you'll want to brush it and clean its ears more often.

1. Brush hair 1 to 2 times weekly

2. Trim nails every 4 to 6 weeks.

3. Unless you have a Texel, you don't really need to bathe your guinea pig. Just make sure to keep its cage and environment clean.

Toys & Playtime

Toys are an important way to keep your pet guinea pig entertained while it is in its cage. We discussed good toys that are safe for guinea pigs in the previous chapter. It is highly recommended that you get a few toys for your pet.

In addition to providing toys, you should ideally let your guinea pig out of its cage so that it can play and exercise in a wider area for at least 1-2 hours per day (the longer, the better).

If you get a play pen for your guinea pig, it's easy to let it play out of its cage without having to constantly supervise it. But if you want it to bond with you, you should make sure to actively play with it on a daily basis.

Common Problems & Illnesses

Before we get into the common health problems, it's important to note that you should always get your guinea pig from a rescue shelter or from a certified breeder. Pet stores are notorious for selling sickly guinea pigs that die within a week or two of being brought home.

Even if a guinea pig seems healthy and happy at the pet store, it could have a serious illness. So it's best to go to a rescue or direct to a breeder where the employees have much more expertise about guinea pigs and can ensure a healthy, strong pet.

Vitamin C Deficiency

Guinea pigs are similar to humans in that neither of us can produce our own vitamin C. We need to get all of it from our diet. So if you are not careful to make sure your guinea pig is getting enough vitamin C, it will be at risk for a deficiency.

To check if your guinea pig has a deficiency, look for swollen joints or internal bleeding. They will be weak, lethargic, and lose their appetite. It will struggle to move since the swollen joints will be painful. They may also experience diarrhea.

Take your guinea pig to the vet if it is experiencing these symptoms.

Ulcerative Pododermatitis

This is a common problem for guinea pigs that are made to walk on hard surfaces or wire mesh floors. This is another reason why the bedding in your cage is so important. It's also why you should absolutely avoid getting a cage with a wire mesh bottom.

The symptoms of this illness include swollen or ulcerated feet. You can avoid this problem by making sure to put plenty of bedding in your guinea pig's cage and making sure to freshen it regularly.

Dental Problems

When guinea pigs don't have enough hay or other materials to chew on, their teeth will start to grow too long. Because their teeth grow continuously, they need to constantly gnaw on things to grind them down.

When their teeth are allowed to get too long, they will have difficulty eating and they may even pierce into their gums or cheeks which can cause pain and infection. It will also make them more prone to dental diseases.

Avoid this problem by making sure your pet's cage is consistently stocked with fresh timothy hay.

Mites Infestation

Due to their long hair, they are a major target for mites which like to burrow into their fur. The symptoms of mites include itchiness, excessive scratching, and hair loss.

This can lead to sleep loss, loss of appetite, and general discomfort. Fortunately, mite infestations are easily treated. You can get special shampoos (similar to lice shampoos) to clean your guinea pig.

If a mite infestation occurs, make sure to remove your guinea pig from its cage to a new location while it is recovering from the infestation. Meanwhile, do a deep cleaning of the cage to remove any infested materials.

Chapter 5: How to Train Your Guinea Pig

Whether you want your new pet to do cool tricks that impress your friends or you just want to make sure it's better behaved and easier to take care of, training your guinea pig is an important part of pet ownership.

Not only will it be better behaved and more responsive to you, you will strengthen your bond with each other as you spend quality time working together during training sessions.

So let your new friend out of the cage and start teaching it some new skills that will make life easier and more entertaining for everyone.

In this chapter, you'll learn the basic method for training your guinea pig to do any trick. You'll also learn the steps to train them how to stay, come, sit, beg, play dead, run in a circle, and even use a litter box!

Basic Commands: Wait, Stay, No

The basic method for training a guinea pig (as with most pets) is to use the following strategy:

1. Choose a treat that you know your guinea pig enjoys such as a piece of fruit.

2. Choose a simple command phrase for the trick you want it to learn such as "wait" or "stay." It should be simple and short and you should make sure this is the only phrase you use when commanding it to do that trick.

3. Say the phrase in a firm voice but do not shout. You want to command its attention, not frighten it.

4. At the beginning, you will have to physically handle the guinea pig in order to make it do the appropriate behavior. For example, with "stay", you will want to physically (but gently) stop it while it is in the middle of moving.

5. Make sure that you use the command phrase before or during the moment in which it does the behavior.

instructions from earlier, do the following to teach this trick:

1. Choose either "sit" or "beg" (or another simple word of your choice).

2. Hold the treat above its head while saying your chosen command word.

3. Allow it to have the treat only when it sits up in the position you want it to be in for this trick.

Repeat this for a few sessions with the treat out. Then, try doing it with just your hand above its head (without a treat). At this time, make sure to have a treat available but hidden so that you can reward your guinea pig for responding to the command.

Eventually, you can get to a point where you don't even have to hold your hand it above it. You can simply say the command word and it will sit up on its hind legs.

Run in Circles

This is one is a fairly simple trick to teach. You'll definitely need a fairly large area to practice it though. Start by holding your treat in front of your guinea pig, far away enough that it needs to walk a few steps in order to reach it.

Once it reaches your hand (but before it gets the treat), move your hand away and to the left (or the right) so that it needs to turn in order to approach your hand again.

Continue doing this until your guinea pig has done a full circle. Then, let it enjoy the treat. Repeat this until the guinea pig is able to do it just by following your hand without a treat and then by just hearing your command phrase.

A good command phrase for something like this would be "circle" or "spin."

Use a Litterbox

You can also teach your guinea pig to use a litterbox. In fact, they will appreciate having a separate place to use the toilet that isn't near their normal living space.

This trick is really only practical if you can provide your guinea pig with a large enough cage or pen that there is room for a small litter box. The obvious advantage of this trick is that the bedding won't get dirty as quickly and you're less likely to get pooped on while holding the guinea pig.

To do it, you should start by placing the litter box inside their cage in the same exact spot that they use as a toilet already. Place a handful of bedding or hay that has been urinated on inside the litterbox. You should also place a few fecal pellets in the litter box as well.

This will help it quickly make the association that this strange new box is where it should be going to the toilet now.

Then, all you have to do is reward it with a treat each time you notice it using the litterbox. Don't punish it when it goes outside of the litterbox. Simply use positive reinforcement when you see that it has used the box correctly.

This one is a slow process as you can't have fixed training sessions. All you can do is wait and pay attention. Eventually, it will get used to the idea and start using the box more and more often.

While you're still training it, make sure that even when you clean the litterbox, you allow a little bit of urine and fecal matter to remain behind so that it can still smell where it should be going to the toilet.

Shake

To teach your guinea pig to shake, you'll first want to teach it to sit up on its hind legs. This way, its front paws are available for shaking. Use a command word like "shake" or "paw" for this trick.

When you first start, say the command word at the same time that you gently grab its paw with your fingers and shake. Then, give it a treat. Repeat this.

After a few sessions of this, you can try holding your finger out while saying the command word to see if it tries to grab your finger. When it does grab your finger, reward it with a treat.

Chapter 6: A Brief Guide to Guinea Pig Breeding

If you are considering breeding guinea pigs, there are a lot of different things you have to consider and many other responsibilities involved that go above and beyond the basic guinea pig care that you have been reading about in the previous chapters of this book.

You need to know how to select a male and female that are suitable for breeding, how to encourage them to breed (rather than fight) and how to care for the female while pregnant as well as the young before they are old enough to be separated from the mother.

You'll learn about all of this and more in this chapter. So this is something you are considering, continue reading.

If you simply want to have 1 or 2 guinea pigs as pets, just make sure you read the part about how to sex them properly and be sure that your pet guinea pigs are the same sex. For keeping as pets, it's best to get 2 females rather than 2 males as they are more likely to get along with each other.

Males may fight each other and getting 2 of the opposite sex will turn you into a guinea pig breeder whether you like it or not! So learning to sex properly is important and a local pet store employee may not have the training or experience to do it properly so it's important that you double check yourself before buying!

Reproduction Facts

Guinea pigs become fertile and capable of reproducing as early as 3 to 5 weeks after births. Females are able to become pregnant all year round but the peak season is in spring.

A pregnancy lasts between 59 to 72 days. The average is between 63 to 68 days. They can have up to 5 litters of guinea pig pups per year. While the female is capable of becoming pregnant again as soon as a few hours after giving birth, it is not healthy for her to repeatedly become impregnated.

It is important to allow her rest time between pregnancies so that she can heal and relax.

She will grow large and sort of eggplant shaped when she is pregnant. One pregnancy can yield anywhere between 1 to 6 guinea pig pups with the average number being three.

Unlike most other rodent species, guinea pig pups are born almost fully developed. They are able to move and eat solid food immediately (although they do still nurse).

Also unlike other rodent species, female guinea pigs living together will help raise pups even if they did not give birth to them. They are known to adopt the pups of others.

Sexing Your Guinea Pig

Male and female guinea pigs look extremely similar. If you are not trying to breed them, it is especially important to be absolutely sure that you are getting two guinea pigs of the same sex.

Because they are so similar, even the pet store employee may not be able to accurately tell the difference. The best way to do this is to gently hold the guinea pig so that its belly faces upward toward you.

Press gently on the fur above its pelvis. If it is a male, a penis will protrude (from near the anus) when gentle pressure is applied. If it is a female this will, obviously, not happen. Do this a few times and look very carefully to make sure you did not miss anything.

Finding Quality Guinea Pig Parents

If you intend to breed guinea pigs and sell them, you need to go to a quality breeder to get your parent guinea pigs. Pet stores are unreliable and often sell sickly or genetically mutated guinea pigs (as a result of incestuous breeding).

Caring for Guinea Pigs during Pregnancy and Birth

During the 2 or so months that your guinea pig is pregnant, you'll want to make sure your female is very comfortable and being fed the highest quality foods. She should be separated from other guinea pigs while she is pregnant.

During the latter weeks of the pregnancy, take care that the temperature stays relatively cool because your female guinea pig will be more prone to death by heat stroke at this stage.

This shouldn't be a problem during cooler months but if she is pregnant during the summer, you'll want to bump up the a/c more regularly for the last couple of weeks.

Avoid picking her up while she is pregnant as they may abort the fetuses if they become alarmed. If you have to pick her up, do it gently, support her hind quarters well and make sure she sees you coming.

The birth will last around 20 minutes. They usually do not need any assistance. It's best to leave them alone. When she's finished, she will remove the amniotic sac and begin to clean off her newborn pups. She will probably eat the placenta.

While the mother is nursing, you should switch from timothy hay to alfalfa hay as they have a higher need for calcium at this time. Once nursing is done, switch both the babies and the mother to timothy hay.

Caring for the Babies

Once the pups are born, you can safely handle them from them immediately. However, it is recommended that your children be kept away from the pups (unless you know you can trust them to be extremely gentle).

Unlike other rodents, the mother will still accept her pups even if you have handled them so this is not a problem. You should try to get them sexed immediately because you will want to separate the males from the females by the third week (when they become sexually mature). The female pups should be left with their mother for at least 4 weeks.

It can take newborns as long as 24 hours to start nursing so don't be concerned about them unless it takes longer than 24 hours. The mother will produce a special fecal stool after birth that is specially designed for the babies to eat. So, again, don't be concerned if you see the babies eating fecal pellets.

Interact with the pups often (but very gently) so that they quickly become socialized to humans. This will make them more desirable pets when you sell them as they will already be friendly and comfortable around humans.

Selling Guinea Pigs

There is a market for quality guinea pigs, especially the longer haired varieties which are often brought to pet shows but for these, you need to be able to guarantee its health, its breeding, and its pedigree. This is yet another reason why you absolutely should not breed with guinea pigs from a pet shop.

To sell them, you can simply start an online business or try to make a deal with local pet shops.

Conclusion

After reading this guide, you have a good idea of what your responsibilities as a guinea pig owner will be. You can figure out whether or not it fits into your budget and your schedule.

More importantly, if you have decided that you will get a guinea pig, you now know exactly what you need to do in order to give it the best life a guinea pig could ask for. You are fully prepared to become a guinea pig owner if you feel it's the right decision for you.

If you are considering breeding, it's advisable to hold off until you get accustomed to caring for just one or two guinea pigs for a while. Start breeding only after you've already got the hang of normal guinea pig care.

As you have already read, caring for pregnant guinea pigs as well as newborns present unique challenges. So it's best to take this one step at a time in order to avoid overwhelming yourself with too much responsibility at once.

With that said, enjoy being the brand new owner of a happy little guinea pig! Keep this book on hand as a reference in case you encounter a problem. This can be the first place you turn in order to decide what to do next.